SO-BED-962

Animals on the Move

by Sue Davies

Harcourt
SCHOOL PUBLISHERS

Cover, p.8, ©W. Perry Conway/CORBIS; p.3, p.9, ©D. Robert & Lorri Franz/CORBIS; p.6, ©Eric and David Hosking/CORBIS; p.7, p.14, ©Corbis; p.10, ©Joe McDonald/CORBIS; p.11, ©Tim Davis/CORBIS; p.12, ©Kevin Fleming/CORBIS; p.13, ©Dewitt Jones/CORBIS.

Cartography, p.5, Joe LeMonnier

Printed in China

ISBN 10: 0-15-350788-8
ISBN 13: 978-0-15-350788-5

Ordering Options
ISBN 10: 0-15-350601-6 (Grade 4 On-Level Collection)
ISBN 13: 978-0-15-350601-7 (Grade 4 On-Level Collection)
ISBN 10: 0-15-357925-0 (package of 5)
ISBN 13: 978-0-15-357925-7 (package of 5)

4 5 6 7 8 9 10 0940 12 11 10 09

It's a late October morning in the Rocky Mountains of northern Wyoming. A herd of mule deer is on a mountain slope. As the snow begins to fall, something happens inside the brains of the deer. So, the herd starts to head down the mountain.

The air feels warmer as they move down the mountain. After crossing the foothills at the bottom, they turn to the south and continue walking. They walk for days. Finally, more than one hundred miles from their home on the mountain, the mule deer stop. They have reached a field of sagebrush. This is where they will stay until the beginning of summer.

The mule deer are *migrating*, or moving to another place. There aren't many plants to eat high in the mountains during the winter. So, mule deer move to a warmer place to find food. Migration helps mule deer and many other animals survive.

Most animals migrate to find food or to avoid a hard season, like winter. They are usually lured to other places by warmer climates. Birds, fish, mammals, and even some insects migrate. Some animals, like mule deer, may migrate a short distance. Others, like zebras, may travel over one thousand miles.

Animals migrate in different ways. Some animals make a round-trip migration each year. This type of migration mimics a human taking a vacation. A person may get on a plane in New York City. They will fly to Florida, stay there for a week, and then fly back home. The "round-trip" airplane ticket takes the person to warm Florida and back. Some animals will live in one place for a while. They migrate to another place for several months, and then return to the first place. The animals that migrate like this tend to do so every year.

ARCTIC OCEAN

Greenland

Hudson Bay

Fall Migration

CANADA

Rocky Mountains

Great Plains

California

UNITED

STATES

Appalachians

New York

Texas

Gulf Coastal Plain

Florida

ATLANTIC OCEAN

Gulf of Mexico

CUBA

Caribbean Sea

N
W E
S

PACIFIC OCEAN

MEXICO

BELIZE

5

Birds migrate more than any other group of animals. In some types of birds, the males and females migrate at different times. When spring comes, the males may leave first. They fly ahead to find a good nesting place. The females leave later and meet the males there.

Shorebirds are small North American birds that live in wetland areas. In the spring, some female shorebirds will leave first. The male shorebirds, who will come later, are left behind to take care of baby birds.

Geese are large birds that mate for life. This means that a male and female goose will always be partners. They always migrate together as part of a group.

Many birds migrate together in huge flocks. Some flocks are so large that they stretch for hundreds of miles. Even birds that live alone may join a flock during migration. One example is predatory birds, such as hawks and falcons. They may travel with a flock of other kinds of birds for hundreds of miles.

Cranes, ducks, pelicans, and geese fly in a formation that resembles the letter *V*. The *V* points in the direction the birds are flying. This helps the flock fly long distances because the birds at the front cut through the air. That makes it easier for the other birds to fly. The birds take turns being the leader.

Different birds fly at different speeds. Ducks, for example, can fly 60 miles per hour (96.5 km). Peregrine falcons fly more than 200 miles (321 km) per hour. Most birds fly faster when they are migrating. Often they fly for six hours or so and then stop to rest. Some birds will stop for several days to eat and rest.

Far more birds migrate than land animals. Why is this so? The answer is deceptively easy: it's much simpler for birds because they can fly. Obviously, flying lets them travel far without a huge effort.

The Arctic tern is a small bird that makes a 22,000 mile (35,405 km) round-trip each year. It takes the tern about ninety days to fly from Antarctica to the Arctic. Imagine how long this journey would take an animal that walks along the ground!

Land animals do migrate. North American animals, such as elk and some sheep, travel to find better feeding areas. Large animals in Africa, such as zebras and wildebeests, travel to find wetter areas based on the rains.

The bat is the only mammal that can fly. This trait makes it easier for bats to migrate. Some bats make short trips in the winter. They move to find more comfortable caves.

Other bats that are larger and stronger travel over longer distances. The silver-haired bat, for example, lives in Canada. Every year it flies all the way to the southern part of the United States. Fruit bats are bats that eat fruit. These bats move to where the fruit is ripe. Then they move to a new place where other fruit is ripe.

Some sea mammals also migrate. They include several kinds of dolphins, porpoises, seals, and whales.

In the winter, many whales move to warmer waters to find more food. Whales that live south of the equator swim north. Whales that live north of the equator swim south. For example, humpback whales that live in the northern Atlantic Ocean swim south to the Caribbean Sea.

Many fish also migrate. Some salmon do so only once in their lives. They do this to lay their eggs. Salmon that live in the Atlantic and Pacific Oceans find the river in which they were born. Then they swim up it, often traveling more than 1,800 miles (2,896 km). Many salmon die after finally reaching the river and laying their eggs. While some kinds of salmon migrate just once, others do so each year.

Perhaps the most famous insect migration is that of the North American monarch butterfly. These beautiful orange and black butterflies fly south in the winter to escape low temperatures. Many monarchs fly to California, Texas, and Florida, where they live in small groups. They fly back north in the summer. Some of these butterflies travel over 3,000 miles (4,828 km) in a single year. They can fly more than 80 miles (128 km) a day!

How do animals know how to find their migration areas? Animals navigate, or find their way, in many different ways. Many animals use landforms, such as rivers, mountain chains, or coastlines.

Some animals navigate by moving in the same direction as the wind. Salmon can tell where they're going by the smell of the river water. Birds can hear the sound of wind blowing over mountains or ocean waves that are hundreds of miles away. Some insects seem to navigate by following certain smells.

Different animals migrate in different ways. Migration is a fascinating example of how animals use their instincts to survive.

Think Critically

1. What causes most animals to migrate?

2. What is a round-trip migration?

3. How are the migrations of many animals alike? How are they different?

4. How can you tell that this book is nonfiction?

5. What are some details in this book that most interested you?

 Science

Look It Up Use a science book or the Internet to find out more about the migration of an animal from this book. Write a paragraph using the information you find.

School-Home Connection Discuss this book with a family member. Then talk about the challenges that animals face daily.

Word Count: 1,115 (1,138)